THE NEW TESTAMENT

— IN —

ITS WORLD WORKBOOK

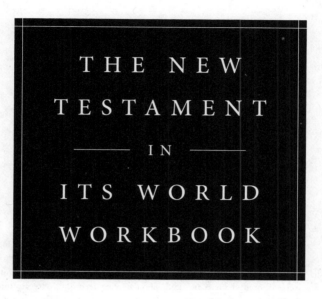

THE NEW TESTAMENT

IN

ITS WORLD WORKBOOK

AN INTRODUCTION TO THE HISTORY,
LITERATURE, AND THEOLOGY OF
THE FIRST CHRISTIANS

N.T. WRIGHT
MICHAEL F. BIRD

First published in Great Britain in 2019
Society for Promoting Christian Knowledge

36 Causton Street
London SW1P 4ST
www.spck.org.uk

Published in North America by Zondervan Academic
an imprint of Zondervan, *3900 Sparks Dr. SE, Grand Rapids, Michigan 49546*

ISBN 978-0-310-52870-8 (softcover)

ISBN 978-0-310-52872-2 (ebook)

British Library Cataloguing-in-Publication Data

A catalogue record for this book is available from the British Library

ISBN 978-0-281-08367-1

Cover design: Brand Navigation
Cover photo: Ruben Ramirez / Unsplash
Interior design: Kait Lamphere

Printed in the United States of America

22 23 24 25 26 27 28 29 /LSC/ 15 14 13 12 11 10 9 8 7 6 5 4

Contents

Part IV
THE RESURRECTION OF THE SON OF GOD

Part V
PAUL AND THE FAITHFULNESS OF GOD

Part VI
THE GOSPELS AND THE STORY OF GOD

Part VII
THE EARLY CHRISTIANS AND THE MISSION OF GOD

Part VIII
THE MAKING OF THE NEW TESTAMENT

Part IX
LIVING THE STORY OF THE NEW TESTAMENT

I

READING THE
NEW TESTAMENT

The Last Supper, dated to the fifteenth century, Novgorod School, National Museum of Russian Art, Kiev

A. Burkatovski / Fine Art Images

Beginning Study of the New Testament

1. Think about a book you have read that has had a deep impact on you, such as a novel, a mystery-thriller, a biography, a real-crime book, a children's book, a history book, a political manifesto, or something in nonfiction. Then answer this question: 'Why did the book have such an impact on me?'

2. Now think about the New Testament, your favourite part of it, the parts you might not know so well, parts that unsettle you, and verses you can recite from memory. Then answer this question: 'Why does the New Testament matter to me, my family, and my church?'

3. In *The New Testament in Its World* we make the following claim:

> The biblical drama is the heaven-and-earth story, the story of God and the world, of creation and covenant, of creation spoiled and covenant broken, and then of covenant renewed and creation restored. The New Testament is the book where all this comes in to land, and it lands in the form of an invitation: this can be and should be *your* story, *my* story, the story which makes sense of us, which restores us to sense after the nonsense of our lives, the story which breathes hope into a world of chaos, and love into cold hearts and lives.

How can studying the New Testament help you make *the biblical* story become *your* story?

4. The New Testament is not just a story we read; it is a story – a drama even – in which we participate. The two main things the New Testament drives us to are w_____p and m_____n.

5. Why study the New Testament? Fill in the blanks from the list of words below.

'The New Testament is designed to draw us into the story of _____, to rescue the world from _____ and _____, and to launch his new transformative _____.'

chaos, God's plan, creation, idolatry

6. What do we lose if we forget that the New Testament is history?

What do we lose if we forget that the New Testament is literature?

What do we lose if we forget that the New Testament is theology?

The New Testament as History

1. What event in the biblical story do you wish you could have witnessed in person?

2. Provide one example of how knowing some historical background helps you better understand something in the New Testament.

3. Discuss one way the ancient world of first-century Judea is very different from your own twenty-first-century context.

4. Why is retrieving and understanding the past fraught with problems?

    a. Sources can be sparse and open to interpretation.

    b. Historians can be biased and project their biases into their research.

    c. Historians need to be aware of diverse sources and various disciplines, including ancient languages and literature, archaeology, sociology, and philosophy.

    d. All of the above.

5. Match the view of history with its description:

modernist view	History is knowable, but it is never known independently of our own interpretation and biases.
postmodernist view	Historical knowledge is possible, objective, and definitive.
critical realist view	There is no true history, only interpretation and ideological agendas in the social science called history.

6. Why is it that 'myth' can never be substituted for 'history' in regard to Christianity? Explain your answer with references to the historical Jesus.

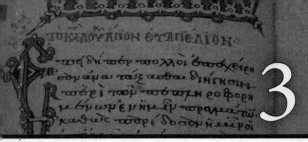

The New Testament as Literature

1. What do you think is the most beautiful part of the New Testament? Maybe the Lord's Prayer, the Sermon on the Mount, Jesus' discussion with the two disciples on the road to Emmaus, Paul's ode to love in 1 Corinthians 13, the 'hall of faith' in Hebrews 11, the throne scene in Revelation 5, or something else?

2. When we say that a text 'means' something, what are we talking about?

    a. What the author *intended* to communicate.

    b. How the text makes *arguments* and *creates* a story.

    c. How readers *respond* to the text.

    d. All of the above.

3. Where is meaning to be found in biblical texts? Fill in the blanks from the list of words below.

It appears that authors _____, texts _____, and readers _____; and that 'meaning' occurs in the _____ of all three. Ultimately, 'meaning' is the web of _____ _____ we make with the world behind the text, the world in the text, and the world we inhabit in front of the text. The more _____ we make, and the thicker those connections appear to be, the more preferable is a particular meaning ascribed to the text because it explains more of the elements involved in the entire reading _____.

understand, cognitive connections, intend, experience, fusion, connections, signify

4. According to Christopher Spinks, 'Meaning is the mediation of God's truth that takes place between authors, readers, and the community of God of which they are all a part. It is neither a determined object nor an open-ended idea.'[*]

AGREE or DISAGREE

Why?

5. What is a 'hermeneutic of love'?

----

* Spinks 2007, 182–83 (from textbook on p. 73).

6. A type of reading known as *lectio catholica semper reformanda* entails which of the following?

    a. A reading that champions the authority of the Bible over the magisterium or managerial class of any church, whether it is Protestant, Catholic, or Orthodox.

    b. A reading of and for and in the whole church, but a reading which is always in need of revising and reforming, even as such readings themselves should revise and reform the church.

    c. A reading that affirms catholic sensibilities about consensus and is sensitive to Protestant suspicions about medieval dogma.

    d. A reading that advocates the competency of every soul or person to interpret the Bible for themselves irrespective of what the church or anyone in church history thinks.

4

The New Testament as Theology

1. Which of the following did the risen Jesus say in Matthew's gospel?

    a. 'All authority is given to the holy books you shall write about me.'
    b. 'All authority is given to Peter and his successors.'
    c. 'All authority in heaven and on earth has been given to me.'
    d. 'All authority belongs to the politicians who sound the most like me.'

2. Why does New Testament theology need *both* historical description *and* theological prescription?

3. If the authority of the New Testament derives from its message, its theology, then what are the central tasks in any exposition of New Testament theology?

4. What makes New Testament theology theological? Fill in the blanks from the list of words below.

New Testament theology plots the _____ that answers, as only stories can, the great worldview questions: _____ _____ _____, where we are, what time it is, what's wrong, what the solution might be, and what we should be doing about it. The church then lives under the 'authority' of the extant story, being required to offer an _____ _____ of the final act of that story as it leads up to and anticipates the intended conclusion.

improvisatory performance, story, who we are

5. How does New Testament theology help churches grow disciples and address the wider world with its message?

II

THE WORLD OF JESUS AND THE EARLY CHURCH

Ethiopian icon of the crucifixion; date and author unknown
Gianni Dagli Orti / Shutterstock

The History of the Jews between the Persian and Roman Empires

1. Match the dates to the time periods for control of Palestine:

Babylonian	142 BC
Persian/Greek	538–320 BC
Egyptian (Ptolemaic)	200–163 BC
Syrian (Seleucid)	597–539 BC
Beginning of Hasmonean Dynasty	320–200 BC

2. On the map below, draw the boundaries of the Macedonian Empire at its height during the reign of Alexander the Great.

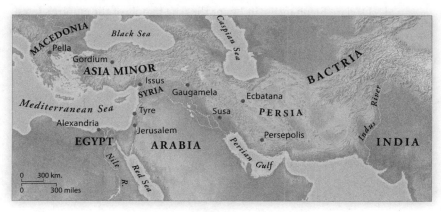

Alexander the Great's Empire

3. What is the name of the Syrian king who desecrated the Jerusalem temple in 167 BC?

    a. Marcus Antonius
    b. Antiochus Magnus
    c. Apocryphal Parmenides
    d. Antiochus IV Epiphanes

4. Number these events according to their chronological order:

    _____ Herod made king of Judea by Romans
    _____ Period of semi-autonomy from Syrian rule
    _____ Hasmonean Dynasty established
    _____ Roman general Pompey intervenes in Hasmonean civil war
    _____ Maccabean revolt
    _____ Parthian invasion of Judea

5. In AD 40 Emperor Gaius Caligula was so enraged by an insult to his divine honour that he ordered the governor of Syria, Publius Petronius, to march into Jerusalem with two legions and to do what?

    a. Read the poems of Virgil to the Sanhedrin.
    b. Erect a golden statue of the emperor in the Jewish temple.
    c. Execute James the brother of Jesus.
    d. Declare Elephantine in Egypt the true temple of the empire's Jews.

6. On the map below, identify by colour the regions bequeathed by Herod the Great to his surviving sons Archelaus (red), Philip (green), and Antipas (blue).

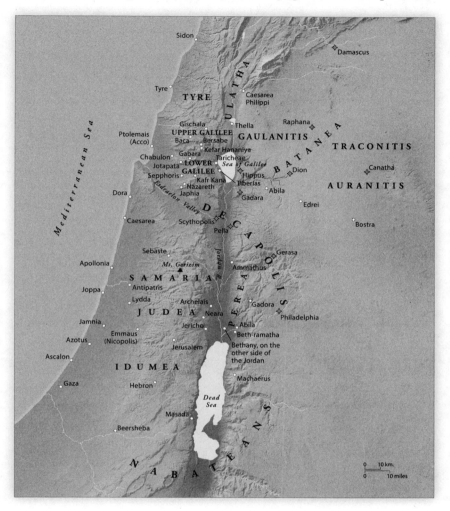

7. The outbreak of the Judean rebellion against Rome was instigated principally by the son of the high priest Eleazar and a band of rogue priests who refused to do what?

    a. Offer sacrifices on behalf of the emperor.

    b. Provide volunteers to serve in the Roman military.

    c. Offer sacrifices to the genius of the emperor.

    d. Clamp down on the Judean People's Front.

8. In what years was the Bar-Kochba revolt waged against the Roman rule of Judea?

9. Can you name all the Roman emperors of the first century? Fill in the blanks from the names of Roman emperors below.

27 BC–AD 14		AD 69	Vitellius
AD 14–37	Tiberius	AD 69–79	
AD 37–41		AD 79–81	Titus
AD 41–54	Claudius	AD 81–96	
AD 54–68		AD 96–98	Nerva
AD 68–69	Galba	AD 98–117	
AD 69			

Gaius Caligula, Otho, Domitian, Augustus, Trajan, Vespasian, Nero

10. The beginning of rabbinic Judaism is normally associated with the council of _____.

6

The Jewish Context of Jesus and the Early Church

1. On the map below, draw the following (see p. 96 of textbook for help if needed):

- Sea of Galilee
- Jordan River
- Dead Sea
- Jerusalem
- Tiberias
- Caesarea Maritima

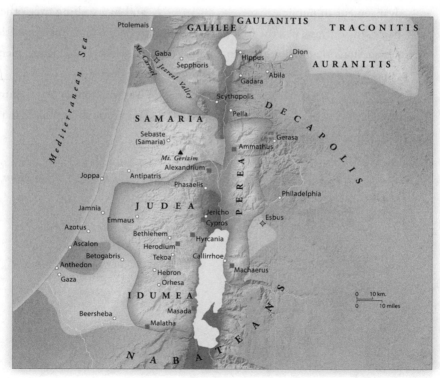

The holy land

2. Number the following according to their social rank and economic means:

___ municipal elites

___ ruling elite

___ low-level merchants

___ destitutes

___ peasants

___ professional class

___ regional elites

3. What was the significance of honour and shame in first-century culture? Fill in the blanks from the list of words below.

Honour was the public _____ of a person's value by peers. Honour in the ancient world could be inherited by a _____ _____, be paid according to one's _____ or social rank, or be acquired through social advancement in public _____ and by excelling over others. Shame, in contrast, was the lack or loss of honour due to one's social position or by actions that caused one to _____ _____ (there are, again, plenty of modern equivalents). For males, honour was acquired by _____ _____, abilities, and trustworthiness; for women, honour was acquired through modesty, _____, and the kind of domestic skills praised in the final chapter of the book of Proverbs.

chastity, accomplishments, showing courage, noble birth, lose face, affirmation, gender

4. The *miqvaot* were _____ used for ritual cleansing.

5. Match the view to the Jewish sect:

zealous groups — 'We only accept Torah as Scripture and reject the idea of resurrection.'

Pharisees — 'We are the "sons of light"; the temple is corrupted, so let's go into the wilderness and wait for God.'

Sadducees — 'Israel's restoration comes through priestly purity, good *halakhah*, and religious zeal.'

Essenes — 'Ingratiate yourself to the Romans and keep the peace at all costs.'

Qumranites — 'We like the ascetic life, we don't own slaves, and we have a gate named after us.'

Herodians — 'No king but God.'

6. The main pillars of Judaism were the following:

M_____: There is only one God of creation and covenant.

E_____: God has chosen Israel to be his special people, his agents in his worldwide purposes.

E_____: We look forward to the return of YHWH to Zion to rescue his people.

7. Briefly describe what the Jews in first-century Palestine hoped God would do for them. What Old Testament text would you use to support your view?

The Greco-Roman Context of the Early Church

1. Name the three instruments that spread Hellenistic culture in the ancient world:

    a. l_____

    b. p_____

    c. r_____ s_____

2. Draw the boundaries of the Roman Empire when it achieved its zenith under Trajan.

Roman Empire

3. The Capitoline hill in Rome was crowned with a temple to the triad of gods including J_____, M_____, and J_____.

4. What was Greco-Roman religion focused on? Fill in the blanks from the list of words below.

Roman 'religion' was largely controlled by the state through a set calendar and the appointment of _____ and vestal virgins. It was practiced both in _____ and in the _____. The private 'household gods' in each home were particularly important, with the father of the family acting as priest. These 'household gods' comprise the _____, small statues of two young men, and the *penates*, the small cult statues placed at the innermost point of the home, symbolizing the identity of a particular family. Harder to describe, but extremely important, was the _____ of the father of the household. The *genius* was the deified concept of the person in his true identity or self. It could be represented with a small statue and was invoked on the occasion of marriage or of oath-taking. Philosophically speaking, the *genius* was the true, spiritual inner core of a person, or indeed of a place; hence the *genius loci*, the 'spirit of a place', which could also be invoked as a _____.

lares, public, priests, genius, divinity, home

5. Match the social tier with the description:

senatorial	members of civil councils in provincial cities
equestrian	property with a soul
decurions	general citizens, owning little farms, workshops, or small businesses
plebeians	ex-slaves, often still in a dependent relationship with their former master
freedman	owned property estimated at 1 million sesterces
slaves	aggregate wealth of around 400,000 sesterces

6. Two prominent books reflecting Greek and Roman culture were the
I_____ by Homer and A_____ by Virgil.

7. List four ways in which ancient religion was different from modern ideas
of 'religion'.*

    a. Concern with p_____ l_____ rather than with an
a_____.

    b. Focused on c_____ r_____ rather than on d_____
b_____.

    c. No s_____ with a s_____ of r_____ and
s_____.

    d. Pluralistic but not necessarily t_____.

8. Of the list that follows, choose the philosophy that had these features:
Pantheistic, sees 'divinity' in everything. World history was based on a
number of repeating cycles, at the end of each of which a great cosmic con-
flagration would purify the world so that its true self would enjoy a time of
stillness before history repeated itself again. Adherents aimed at continual
moral enlightenment with the goal of becoming a genuinely wise and well-
formed person, attaining self-mastery and living in accordance with nature.

    a. Epicureanism
    b. Stoicism
    c. Aristotelianism
    d. Cynicism
    e. existentialism

9. Explain in a hundred words or less the significance of the Jewish diaspora for
the spread of Christianity.

---

* The question is developed from material mostly drawn from Ehrman 2004, 22–8.

III

JESUS AND THE
VICTORY OF GOD

The Mosaic of Jesus, dated 532–7, in the Hagia Sophia ('Holy Wisdom'),
Istanbul, Turkey
Artur Bogacki / Shutterstock

8

The Study of
the Historical Jesus

1. In what way is the historical Jesus, the real Jesus, different from the Jesus of culture, politics, or movies?

2. Why should Christians want to study the historical Jesus?

3. Match the quest with its portrayal of Jesus.

First quest for historical Jesus

Glimmer of optimism about finding Jesus behind the gospels, constrained by form criticism, largely skeptical of authenticity of most materials in the gospels, Jesus becomes either an existentialist or an American West Coast liberal.

No quest period

Jesus was unlike how the gospels portray him, not a God-man but God-conscious, spiritual rather than religious, and fitting somewhere between the philosophical poles of the great German thinkers G. W. F. Hegel and Immanuel Kant.

Second quest for historical Jesus

New insights from archaeology, philology, and sociology in the illumination of Jesus and his context. Working with a better view of ancient Judaism. Taking the Jewishness of Jesus with seriousness. Identify Jesus as eschatological prophet and/or Messiah.

Third quest for historical Jesus

Belief that questing for Jesus was either impossible or illegitimate, even if a few never gave up researching Jesus and the gospels with historical sensitivity.

4. Why does the historical Jesus matter for the origins of Christianity? Fill in the blanks from the list of words below.

One must pursue the question as to why Christianity began, why it took the
_____ that it did, why the gospels are _____ they are, why the first
Christians _____ and _____ as they did, and how all that
relates to the first-century figure Jesus of Nazareth. Christianity is, to some
extent at least, the _____ history of Jesus, the resounding echo of

his influence on his closest _____ and on the movement that con-
sciously identified itself as _____ to him. To outline the history of early
Christianity without engaging in a study of the historical Jesus makes about as
much sense as plotting the history of modern _____ without bothering
to take into account the life and times of Gandhi.

India, believed, disciples, what, shape, acted, devoted, effective

5. Consider this statement:

The point of having Jesus at the centre of a religion or a faith is that one has
Jesus: not a cypher, a strange silhouetted Christ-figure, nor an icon, but the
one Jesus the New Testament writers know, the one born in Palestine in the
reign of Augustus Caesar, and crucified outside Jerusalem in the reign of his
successor, Tiberius. If we close down that historical referentiality, or simply
assume it, without getting our hands dirty in textual and historical exca-
vation, we cease to read the gospels as they were intended, as historically
rooted witnesses to Jesus as told by his disciples.

AGREE or DISAGREE

Why?

9

The Profile and Praxis of a Prophet

1. What verse or cluster of verses from the gospels do you think best summarizes Jesus' message? Provide a one-sentence justification for your answer.

2. Why did Herod Antipas have John the Baptist executed?

3. As a prophet, how was Jesus like some of the biblical prophets of old? Match each prophet to the correct description.

Ezekiel	Jesus constantly ran the risk of being called a traitor to Israel's national aspirations, while claiming all the time that he was nevertheless the true spokesman for the covenant God.
Jeremiah	Jesus taught that the 'Day of the Lord' would be one of darkness not triumph.
Jonah	Jesus performed miracles and gave oracles of judgment.
Amos	Jesus predicted that the temple would be abandoned by the shekinah, left unprotected to its fate.
Elijah	Jesus predicted imminent judgment on Israel and declared that a dramatic sign would validate his message.

4. What did the kingdom of God mean for first-century Jews? Fill in the blanks from the list of words below:

The One God would _____ Israel in a whole new way, _____ in power and glory to rescue his people, rebuke the wicked, and set up a new rule of justice and _____. 'Kingdom of God' meant that _____ would be fulfilled at last, that the _____ would be rebuilt and the _____ cleansed. Israel's God would rule in the way he always intended, through properly appointed persons and means.

temple, returning, land, peace, rule, Torah

5. What did Jesus proclaim in the 'Nazareth Manifesto' of Luke 4.16–21?

    a. The love of God and the brotherhood of man with a view to creating an egalitarian utopia of gender equality, eco-harmony, and redistribution of wealth.

    b. The right to carry arms and form militias, to create one nation under God, and to bring back family values, with a view to ending Roman taxes and tyranny.

    c. The Isaianic signs of deliverance were being manifested as evidenced by the publication of good news for the poor, the release of prisoners from captivity, and the recovery of sight for the blind.

    d. The essence of true religion as a consciousness of God, the compatibility of all religions with each other, and the kingdom of God representing humanity's combined efforts to achieve unity and oneness.

6. Why did Jesus believe that the temple would be destroyed as God's judgment upon it?

10

Who Did Jesus Think He Was?

1. If someone asked you 'Who is Jesus?' what would you say? Explain your answer.

2. Write down six titles used to describe Jesus in the gospels.

a. M_____

b. S_____ o___ M_____

c. S_____ o___ G_____

d. L_____

e. R_____

f. P_____

3. Read this statement:

The adage has been that Jesus was a prophet who claimed to speak for God, and then later the church proclaimed Jesus as God. The man became the message. In response it should be said: Yes, Jesus spoke about God, but as one who had a unique relationship with God. Yes, Jesus spoke about God's kingdom, but as one who had a unique role in ushering it in and ultimately reigning over it. Jesus talked about God's coming kingdom *in order to explain what he himself was doing*. Thus, in contrast to several wings of scholarship, we propose that – once we understand the great stories that the first-century Jewish world knew, and that he was regularly invoking – Jesus' self-understanding is in principle knowable; and there are good reasons for thinking that Jesus thought of himself as taking the key role in the eschatological drama that was beginning to unfold upon Israel.

AGREE or DISAGREE

Why?

4. 'Son of Man' refers to what?

    a. A Hebrew idiom for 'human being'.

    b. An Aramaic idiom of self-reference for 'I' or 'someone in my position'.

    c. A mysterious figure from Daniel 7 who represents God, God's reign, and God's people.

    d. All of the above.

5. All Jews were anxiously waiting for the Messiah to redeem them from Roman oppression.

TRUE or FALSE

Explain your answer.

6. If being the Messiah were a crime, what evidence would there be to convict Jesus?

7. Describe one text, perhaps from Luke's gospel, where Jesus could be regarded as believing that in his own person, YHWH was returning to Zion.

8. Note these words from Mark 14.62: "'I am,' replied Jesus, "and you will see the Son of Man sitting at the right hand of Power and coming with the clouds of heaven"' (authors' translation). What two Old Testament texts are alluded to in Jesus' reply to Caiaphas?

  a. _____
  b. _____

What do they have in common?

11

The Death of the Messiah

1. Do you have a favourite piece of artwork that portrays the crucifixion? If so, what is it, and why do you like it?

2. Was Jesus' death a miscalculation by him, the only reason why he was born, or the climax to his kingdom message? Explain your answer.

3. Why was Jesus crucified? Fill in the gaps from the words below.

   a. Because many saw him as 'a _____ _____, leading Israel astray'.

   b. Because they saw his _____ _____ as a blow against the central symbol not only of national life but also of YHWH's presence with his people and promises for their deliverance.

   c. Because he saw himself as in some sense Messiah and could become a focus of serious _____ _____.

d. Because he was perceived to be a dangerous _____ _____, whose actions might well call down the wrath of Rome upon temple and nation alike.

e. Because, at the crucial moment in the hearing, he not only pleaded guilty to the above charges, but also did so in such a way as to place himself, blasphemously, alongside the _____ ____ _____.

revolutionary activity, God of Israel, temple action, false prophet, political nuisance

4. When Jesus wanted his disciples to understand the meaning of his death, he didn't give them a lecture, a sermon, a manuscript, a letter, a poem, or a song; rather, he gave them a m_____to help them remember his death and to help them understand its significance.

5. The Last Supper deliberately invokes the story of Israel and what?

    a. The Maccabean crisis.
    b. The wilderness wanderings.
    c. The Roman annexation of Judea.
    d. The Passover.

6. What Old Testament texts did Jesus invoke when explaining the significance of his death?

    a. Isaiah 53
    b. Psalm 22
    c. Zechariah 13
    d. all of the above

7. How does Jesus' death relate to the end of exile, the forgiveness of sins, and the defeat of evil?

IV

THE RESURRECTION OF THE SON OF GOD

The *Averoldi Polyptych* by Titian, dated 1520–2, located in the basilica church of Santi Nazaro e Celso, Brescia, Italy

© *Mondadori Electa / Bridgeman Images*

The Afterlife in Greek, Roman, and Jewish Thought

1. Which of these views of the afterlife is *not* generally attributable to Greeks and Romans in antiquity?

    a. Existing as shades in Hades.
    b. Immortality of the soul.
    c. Resurrection.
    d. Divinization (apotheosis).
    e. Entering paradise.
    f. Reincarnation.

2. Why was resurrection an alien and abhorrent concept to Greeks and Romans?

3. The Old Testament has no hint of the resurrection of the body.

TRUE or FALSE

Explain your answer.

4. Match the biblical passage with its contents:

Psalm 16.9–11

'I will deliver this people from the power of the grave; I will redeem them from death. Where, O death, are your plagues? Where, O grave, is your destruction? I will have no compassion, even though he thrives among his brothers.' (NIV)

Hosea 13.14–15

'Multitudes who sleep in the dust of the earth will awake: some to everlasting life, others to shame and everlasting contempt. Those who are wise will shine like the brightness of the heavens, and those who lead many to righteousness, like the stars for ever and ever.' (NIV)

Daniel 12.2–3

But your dead will live, LORD; their bodies will rise – let those who dwell in the dust wake up and shout for joy – your dew is like the dew of the morning; the earth will give birth to her dead. (NIV)

Isaiah 26.19

Therefore my heart is glad and my tongue rejoices; my body also will rest secure, because you will not abandon me to the realm of the dead, nor will you let your faithful one see decay. You make known to me the path of life; you will fill me with joy in your presence, with eternal pleasures at your right hand. (NIV)

5. What Jewish writing from the intertestamental period tells the story of a mother and her seven sons who refuse to obey the king's edict to eat unclean food and are tortured one by one? As they go to their various gruesome deaths, several of them make specific promises to their torturers about the form of their divine vindication, resurrection, that God promises them in the future. Give the book name and chapter number.

6. What role did resurrection have in prophetic hopes about the future?

    a. Resurrection was a way of talking about the *immortality of the soul* and the hope of an eternal *disembodied bliss*.

    b. Resurrection was about the *restoration of Israel* on the one hand and *the newly embodied life of all YHWH's people* on the other.

    c. Resurrection was a call for *political revolution*, to turn the pagan world upside down, by motivating martyrs with the *promise of paradise* in the hereafter.

7. In light of Ezekiel 37 and Revelation 20, how is resurrection a political hope for God's people, not just a pleasant prospect of life after death?

13

The Story of Easter according to the Apostle Paul

1. Ordinarily we think of Paul as the theologian of the cross. While that is certainly true, in what way was Paul also the theologian of the resurrection?

2. How did Paul show the significance of the resurrection for the early church? Fill in the blanks from the list of words below.

    a. It showed the _____ of belief in Jesus' resurrection among Jesus' own circle of disciples.

    b. Paul's _____ to his own encounter with the risen Jesus.

    c. How resurrection, something _____ in Judaism, became _____ in Christianity.

    d. How 'resurrection' as a _____ for Israel's socio-political restoration was deployed as a metaphor for _____ in the Messiah's life-giving power.

metaphor, marginal, participation, testimony, origin, central

3. In light of Philippians 3.20–21, it is more proper to say that Paul believed that the body will be t_____, not a_____.

4. Match the passages from Romans with the correct references:

1.3–4

How much more, in that case – since we have been declared to be in the right by his blood – are we going to be saved by him from God's coming anger! When we were enemies, you see, we were reconciled to God through the death of his son; if that's so, how much more, having already been reconciled, shall we be saved by his life.

4.25

So, then, if the spirit of the one who raised Jesus from the dead lives within you, the one who raised the Messiah from the dead will give life to your mortal bodies, too, through his spirit who lives within you.

5.9–10

The good news about his son, who was descended from David's seed in terms of flesh, and who was marked out powerfully as God's son in terms of the spirit of holiness by the resurrection of the dead: Jesus, the king, our Lord!

6.4–5

If you profess with your mouth that Jesus is Lord, and believe in your heart that God raised him from the dead, you will be saved.

8.11

That means that we were buried with him, through baptism, into death, so that, just as the Messiah was raised from the dead through the father's glory, we too might behave with a new quality of life. For if we have been planted together in the likeness of his death, we shall also be in the likeness of his resurrection.

8.34

That is why the Messiah died and came back to life, so that he might be Lord both of the dead and of the living.

10.9

He was handed over because of our trespasses and raised because of our justification.

14.9

Who is going to condemn? It is the Messiah, Jesus, who has died, or rather has been raised; who is at God's right hand, and who also prays on our behalf!

5. Match the argument summaries with the references from 1 Corinthians 15:

15.1–11	The gospel is anchored in the resurrection of Jesus.
15.12–19	If the resurrection were *not* true, then the central nerve of Christian living would be cut.
15.20–28	The resurrection is about the transformation of present corruptible physicality, resulting in the victory of life over death.
15.29–34	The resurrection body is a new and glorious body, of which risen Jesus' body is the prototype.
15.35–49	Jesus' resurrection is the beginning of 'the resurrection of the dead', the final eschatological event.
15.50–58	If the resurrection did not happen, then the gospel, with all its benefits, is null and void.

6. In 1 Corinthians 15, Paul contrasted what?

a. A body with an *imprisoned soul*, with a body comprised of an *invisible and permeable Spirit*, then living with God in endless eternity.

b. A body *animated by a soul*, a natural life force, with a body *animated by the Spirit*, God's divinely imparted vitalizing power.

c. A body *infested with demonic powers*, with a body resembling *angelic beings*, to bring about a revolution on earth and a renovation of all creation.

7. How would Paul respond to someone who said that they looked forward to living in heaven for eternity?

14

The Story of Easter according to the Evangelists

1. What is your favourite Easter story from the gospels? Why?

2. What is the evidence for the resurrection? Fill in the gaps from the list of words below.

    a. The stories lack scriptural _____.

    b. The burial of Jesus and the discovery of the empty tomb can be regarded as historically _____. The testimony of _____ was considered _____, and people would be unlikely to invent the notion of women as key witnesses if they were making stuff up.

    c. The Easter narratives seem to reflect a mixture of eyewitness _____ and strange _____ as to what actually happened.

    d. The wide _____ of people who saw Jesus is also telling.

    e. We have to wrestle with why the early church said, 'Jesus is risen,' if all they had intended to describe was a _____, a _____, or a vague belief that Jesus had ascended post-mortem into some heavenly, otherworldly realm.

enthusiasm, vision, women, solid, embellishment, hallucination, bewilderment, breadth, spurious

3. Match each description with the correct gospel:

Matthew

This gospel, in its extant form, ends on the notes of fear and trembling, but might well have contained additional material about the Son of Man being raised from the dead and appearing to the disciples, all as further proof of Jesus as the divinely sent prophet who opposed the Jerusalem temple.

Mark

The evangelist has written, through and through, a book of Jewish history and theology. His whole thesis is that Israel's God has been at work in Jesus, a point proved climactically and decisively by his resurrection. This evangelist believed, every bit as much as did Paul, that Jesus really did rise from the dead, leaving an empty tomb behind him, and that he was now invested with all authority in heaven and on earth.

Luke

The gospel's narrative is comparatively more dramatic and more laden with deeper symbolism than the synoptic accounts. The evangelist provides a breathtaking synthesis of theological testimony, early tradition, apostolic memory, and vibrant metaphor, unmatched elsewhere in the New Testament. This gospel ends with new-found faith, but it is faith that must now go out into a new world, a risky resurrection faith facing a new day, and must attempt new tasks without knowing in advance where it all will lead.

John

The evangelist's whole oeuvre is designed, at a large scale, to tell the story of Jesus and the early church in such a way that its position at the climax of Israel's scriptural story can be fully understood and appropriated. Disciples are to understand the Scriptures in a whole new way, in the light of the events that have happened to Jesus. They are to make this fresh reading of Scripture the source of their inner life of burning zeal and their framework for understanding who Jesus was and is, who they are in relation to him, and what they must do as a result.

4. What does the resurrection tell us about the following:

    a. God:

    b. The kingdom of God:

    c. Jesus:

    d. The church:

5. If you had to tweet the story of the resurrection, what would you write? Write your response below in 280 characters.

V

PAUL AND THE FAITHFULNESS OF GOD

Marco Zoppo, *St Paul*, dated 1470, Ashmolean Museum, Oxford
Public Domain

15

The Story of Paul's Life and Ministry

1. Some think of Paul as the hero of Christianity, but for others he's the villain of Christianity. Some see him as a complex figure, somewhere between religious genius and deeply flawed individual. Who is Paul to you?

2. If we didn't have Paul's letters, how would Christianity be different?

3. Match the sentence endings to the proper beginnings:

<table>
<tr><td>Paul's Jewish name was</td><td>Jewish diaspora.</td></tr>
<tr><td>Paul was born in</td><td>artisan class.</td></tr>
<tr><td>Paul trained as a</td><td>Roman citizenship.</td></tr>
<tr><td>Paul grew up within the</td><td>Pharisee.</td></tr>
<tr><td>Paul, as a tentmaker, belonged to the</td><td>Saul.</td></tr>
<tr><td>Paul was born with</td><td>Tarsus.</td></tr>
</table>

4. Why did Paul persecute the church?

a. For believing that a crucified Galilean was the Messiah, which turned the story of Israel on its head.

b. For rehearsing Jesus' critique of the temple and reinterpretation of the Torah.

c. For venerating Jesus in ways that transgressed upon the worship of YHWH.

d. For being religious deviants, rivals to the Pharisees, and for fraternizing with gentiles and leading Israel astray.

e. Out of his zeal for Israel's purity and holiness.

f. All of the above.

5. Match each passage with the correct reference:

Galatians 1.15–16

But when God, who set me apart from my mother's womb, and called me by his grace, was pleased to unveil his son in me, so that I might announce the good news about him among the nations – immediately I did not confer with flesh and blood.

1 Corinthians 9.1

And, last of all, as to one ripped from the womb, he appeared even to me.

1 Corinthians 15.8

Because the God who said 'let light shine out of darkness' has shone in our hearts, to produce the light of the knowledge of the glory of God in the face of Jesus the Messiah.

2 Corinthians 4.6

I'm a free man, aren't I? I'm an apostle, aren't I? I've seen Jesus our Lord, haven't I?

6. On the map below draw the locations of the following places:

- Jerusalem
- Damascus
- Syrian Antioch
- Pisidian Antioch

- Ephesus
- Philippi
- Thessalonica
- Athens

- Corinth
- Troas

7. Name two proconsuls that Paul encountered in his travels according to Acts.

a. _____

b. _____

8. Fill in the gaps in the chronological table from the list below.

ROMANS

Paul in Tarsus; brought to Antioch by Barnabas

Claudius expels Jews from Rome

GALATIANS

Birth of Saul of Tarsus

Death of Paul

Voyage to Rome; shipwreck on Malta

Death of Claudius; accession of Nero

Paul and Barnabas on first missionary journey: Cyprus and South Galatia

Jesus revealed to Saul on road to Damascus

House arrest in Rome

Paul in Corinth

Paul in Ephesus

ca. AD 5–10	
30	Crucifixion and resurrection of Jesus of Nazareth
33	
33–36	Paul in Damascus, Arabia, Damascus again
36	Paul's first post-Damascus visit to Jerusalem (Gal 1.18–24)
36–46	
47–48	
48	Peter in Antioch (Gal 2.11–21); crisis in Galatia
48	
48/49	Jerusalem conference (Acts 15)
49	

(cont.)

49	Paul and Silas on second missionary journey: Greece
50/51	1 and 2 THESSALONIANS
51–52	
52/53	Paul in Jerusalem, Antioch, third missionary journey: Ephesus
53–56	
53	1 CORINTHIANS
53/54	Short, painful visit to Corinth
54	
55	PHILIPPIANS
55/56	PHILEMON, COLOSSIANS, EPHESIANS
56	Released from prison; continues journey to Corinth
56	2 CORINTHIANS
57	
57	From Corinth to Jerusalem
57–59	'Hearings' and imprisonment in Jerusalem and Caesarea
59, autumn	
60, early	Arrival in Rome
60–62	
62–64	Further travels, either to Spain or to the East, or both?
After 62	1 & 2 TIMOTHY & TITUS?
64	Fire of Rome; persecution of Christians in Rome
64 or later	

16

A Primer on Pauline Theology

1. What would you say was Paul's most distinctive teaching?

2. Explain why Philemon represents a useful starting point for understanding Paul's idea of 'theology'.

3. Paul's species of monotheism was not merely philosophical or pantheistic; rather, it was c_____ and c_____.

4. Which definition best describes Paul's monotheism?

    a. The one God of Israel made the world and then left humans alone to find the divine spark within themselves; and this one God, aloof as he or she is, interacts with the world only through angelic messengers.

    b. The one God of Israel made the world and has remained in dynamic relationship with it; and this one God, in order to further his purposes within and for that world, has entered into covenant with Israel in particular.

    c. The one God of Israel is a luminous monad who created the world from a prior world; God allows souls to sojourn upon earth for a while, thereafter to return to heaven before beginning the next cycle of existence, and souls that are especially noble and virtuous are chosen to live among the people of Israel for a time.

5. What two passages from Paul's letters demonstrate how monotheism has been recast around Jesus because Jesus' first followers, like the apostle Paul, found themselves not only permitted to use God-language for Jesus but compelled to use Jesus-language for the one God.

    a. _____

    b. _____

6. What did Paul think of the Holy Spirit? Fill in the blanks from the list of words below.

Across Galatians 4 and Romans 8, Paul was again working from within the _____ of Jewish-style monotheism. He saw the Spirit _____ the Son as the _____ of the one God, doing what _____ was to do, doing what _____ wanted to do but could not.

alongside, Torah, Wisdom, agents, framework

7. Paul regularly spoke of the Spirit in ways which indicate that he regarded the Spirit, as he regarded the Messiah, as the glorious manifestation of YHWH himself. Name two passages which indicate this:

a. _____

b. _____

8. Which view better describes Paul's view of election?

a. The One creator God's special call of Israel and its associated covenantal vocation had been fulfilled through Jesus precisely as Israel's messianic representative, and those purposes were now being implemented through his people, the church. So the Jewish view of election is brought into fresh focus, rethought, reimagined, and reworked around Jesus himself, specifically, his death, resurrection, and enthronement.

b. The one creator God had called gentiles to replace Israel as his special people, and as part of that call, he expected them to live *in* the Spirit and to be obedient *to* Christ.

c. The one creator God has predestined individuals to salvation based on an eternal contract between the Father and Son whereby the Father would permit creatures to fall into sin and the Son would in turn pay for their sin and purchase their eternal redemption.

17

Galatians

1. Draw the emoji which you think best captures Paul's mood when he wrote Galatians.

2. On the map below, draw "political" Galatia.

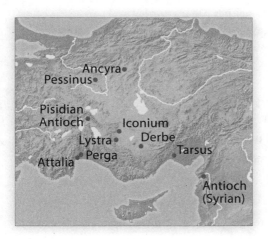

3. Circle your answer. Galatians was written:

Before / After the Jerusalem Council

To the church in North / South Galatia

4. Describe the circumstances that led Paul to write the letter to the Galatians.

5. Why did the 'agitators' want the Galatians to be circumcised?

    a. The church is a messianic chapter of Israel, and the normal rites of entry for proselytes were still in force.

    b. Gentile believers were claiming membership in the family of Israel, despite being uncircumcised, and this was creating havoc for the reputation of the Jerusalem church.

    c. The intruders wanted the Galatians to be circumcised to resolve their ambiguous position as neither pagans nor Jews.

    d. One or more of the above.

6. A summary of Galatians is:

Paul insisted that *you do not have to become physically Jewish to belong to the Messiah's family* – and if you try to do so, you are denying the crucified and risen Messiah himself. God saves gentiles by making them Messiah-people, not by making them Jews – a paradox, of course, but it is precisely the paradox of the crucified and risen Messiah. It was always God's plan, Paul insisted, to have a multi-ethnic family; that is the story scripture tells. That is why the Messiah died and rose. If 'righteousness', that is, the status of being forgiven and possessing a right standing within the covenant, could be gained or validated by means of observing Torah, the Jewish law, then the Messiah died for nothing.

AGREE or DISAGREE

Why?

7. Write out the structure of Galatians.

8. What verse from Galatians do you think best summarizes the letter?

18

1 and 2 Thessalonians

1. What part of 1 and 2 Thessalonians is most memorable to you? Why?

2. Draw Macedonia on the map and locate the city of Thessalonica along the Via Egnatia.

Thessalonica

3. What segment of Acts refers to Paul's ministry in Thessalonica?

4. Two problems that Paul dealt with in these letters are:

    a. _____

    b. _____

5. Why did Paul write 1 Thessalonians? Fill in the gaps from the list of words below.

Paul wrote 1 Thessalonians to praise the little struggling church for their _____ (1 Thess 1.3, 8; 2.13–16; 3.2–13), assuring them that people who _____ in faith would not miss out on _____ in Christ's return, because the 'dead in Christ will rise first' (1 Thess 4.13–5.3). He exhorted them to continue in _____ and godliness in a world of darkness (1 Thess 4.1–12; 5.4–8, 12–22) so that they would be found '_____' at the coming of the Lord Jesus (1 Thess 3.13; 5.23).

participating, blameless, died, perseverance, holiness

6. Why did Paul write 2 Thessalonians? Fill in the gaps from the list of words below.

Paul wrote 2 Thessalonians, addressing these matters of persecution, rumors that the 'Day of the Lord' had already happened, and the problem of people not wanting to work, stressing the importance of remaining _____ and _____ in the face of persecution (2 Thess 1.4, 11–12; 2.15–17; 3.5). They were to remember what they were _____ (2 Thess 2.5, 15; 3:7, 10), and were to live up to the standard implied by, and inherent in, God's _____ (2 Thess 1.5, 11). They were to _____, above all, in the hope of sharing in the glory of the Lord Jesus (2 Thess 2.14).

call, steadfast, rejoice, taught, strong

7. Write an outline of 1 and 2 Thessalonians.

19

Philippians

1. Philippians is considered a letter of joy. What is so joyous about this letter?

2. Philippians quiz.

    a. What famous battle took place at Philippi in 42 BC?

    b. What name did Octavian give to the city?

    c. What was the approximate population of Philippi in Paul's day?

    d. What segment of Acts describes Paul's ministry in Philippi?

e. What two women did Paul write to in 4.2?

f. Which man was from Philippi – Epaphras or Epaphroditus?

3. Paul wrote Philippians from which city?

    a. Caesarea
    b. Ephesus
    c. Rome
    d. Troas
    e. none of the above

4. What are the main purposes of Philippians?

    a. To express gratitude for the financial support arriving through Epaphroditus.
    b. To urge the church to unity in Christ, especially two warring women.
    c. To warn the Philippians about Jewish Christian proselytizers who may turn up.
    d. To update the Philippians on Paul's situation.
    e. All of the above.

5. Who are the 'dogs' (Phil 3.2) that Paul was worried might arrive in Philippi?

6. How is Paul's letter to Philemon different from Pliny's letter to Sabinianus?

7. The household codes of Colossians 3.18–4.1 and Ephesians 5.21–6.9 are directly applicable today.

AGREE or DISAGREE

Why?

8. What better sums up the view of the church in Ephesians?

   a. The church is extrinsic to the work of redemption, the reality of the gospel is spiritual not empirical, the unity among the saints is invisible not institutional, for God intends to reign in the hearts of believers and not in pews, buildings, or committee meetings.
   b. The united church is not an optional extra to the work of redemption, but is itself part of the reality of the gospel, the way in which God is taking forward his plan for the whole cosmos to radiate with his glory.

9. Write an outline of Ephesians.

21

1 and 2 Corinthians

1. Is your church like the church in Corinth? Check the appropriate boxes.

- ☐ People brag about who they were baptized by.
- ☐ The church is characterized by factions and divisions.
- ☐ Some folks think the apostle Paul was not all that impressive in person.
- ☐ Some claim to have superior amounts of wisdom and spiritual gifts compared to everyone else.
- ☐ A man is in a relationship with his stepmother, and most people are okay with it.
- ☐ Rich members are filing lawsuits against poorer members.
- ☐ Some people are advocating lifelong celibacy and singleness.
- ☐ Some people are eating meat that has been offered to pagan deities.
- ☐ Some people are attending restaurants/houses of worship/brothels.
- ☐ Men are praying like pagans, and married women are dressing in culturally immodest ways.
- ☐ Rich members have a fellowship meal early and leave only scraps for the rest of the church.
- ☐ Members are fighting over which spiritual gift is the greatest.
- ☐ Some people are denying a future resurrection.
- ☐ Some people are conducting vicarious baptisms on behalf of the dead.
- ☐ The church is a bit tardy taking up a collection for the poor.
- ☐ People calling themselves 'super-apostles' have arrived and claim they can do a better job than Paul or any of his friends.

2. Corinthians quiz.

    a. In what year was Corinth destroyed by the Romans? _____

    b. In what year was Corinth rebuilt by the Romans? _____

    c. Before the reign of Hadrian, most inscriptions in Corinth were in L_____ whereas most of the graffiti was in G_____.

    d. What year did Paul arrive in Corinth? _____

    e. Who was proconsul when Paul arrived in Corinth? _____

    f. Name three household leaders mentioned in the Corinthian letters. S_____, C_____, and C_____.

    g. What segment of Acts talks about Paul's ministry in Corinth? _____

    h. Which of the following people were *not* members of the Corinthian churches: Gaius, Phoebe, Erastus, Quartus, Arcadius, Tertius, Stephanus, Chloe, Crispus, Sosthenes?

3. Number the events in chronological order:

1	Paul left Corinth.
	These problems were compounded by new moral challenges. Paul learned about all this when he arrived back in Ephesus from Syria. He subsequently wrote a letter to Corinth, urging the church not to associate with believers who engaged in blatant sexual immorality.
	Things then got worse. Timothy brought news that his instructions had not been heeded. Paul therefore made a second visit to Corinth, probably sailing straight across from Ephesus; he referred to this later as a 'painful visit', since he was clearly rebuffed.
	The Corinthians were visited by Apollos, a Greek-speaking Jewish Christian and associate of Aquila and Priscilla and maybe even Peter, passing through Corinth on his way to Rome. These visitors, while good for the church in general, seem to have divided the loyalties of the congregation and generated the beginnings of a personality cult.
	Paul then wrote the much longer letter we call 1 Corinthians, from Ephesus in around AD 53, and sent it through one of the house church leaders who had visited him.
	Titus, however, came from Corinth to meet Paul in Macedonia, and reported both good news and bad news. On the good side, the Corinthians had dealt with the leading antagonist who was fomenting opposition to Paul; the Corinthians had reaffirmed their affection for their original apostle.* On the negative side, Titus also informed Paul of the arrival of the people Paul called 'super-apostles', who had disparaged Paul's ministry as inferior to their own.
	After his release from prison, Paul travelled back to Corinth the long way, by land, around northern Greece, anxious through the first half of the journey about what reception he might expect.
	Paul returned to Ephesus, where the situation deteriorated and ended up with him not only in prison but in seriously bad shape personally and physically. He then may have written what he called a 'letter of tears', which had a powerful effect on the Corinthian church.
9	Paul then wrote 2 Corinthians from Macedonia.

* 2 Corinthians 7.6–16.

4. Match each letter with its description:

Earlier letter

1 Corinthians

'Letter of tears'

2 Corinthians

The letter celebrates the Corinthians' reconciliation to him, gives instructions for a further visit from Titus to get the collection money ready, addresses the question of the 'super-apostles', and prepares them for his third visit.

'I wrote to you in my letter not to associate with sexually immoral people – not at all meaning the people of this world who are immoral, or the greedy and swindlers, or idolaters. In that case you would have to leave this world.' (1 Cor 5.9–10 NIV)

First, Paul wanted to answer several written questions from the Corinthians about marriage and celibacy, food sacrificed to idols, spiritual gifts, the collection, and the prospect of Apollos's return. Second, Paul also wrote in response to disconcerting news from Apollos and several church leaders about factions, incest, lawsuits, women inappropriately dressed, disorder in worship, and particularly (and for Paul crucially) denials of the resurrection.

'Even if I caused you sorrow by my letter, I do not regret it. Though I did regret it – I see that my letter hurt you, but only for a little while – yet now I am happy, not because you were made sorry, but because your sorrow led you to repentance. For you became sorrowful as God intended and so were not harmed in any way by us. Godly sorrow brings repentance that leads to salvation and leaves no regret, but worldly sorrow brings death' (2 Cor 7.8–10 NIV).

5. Write an outline of 1 Corinthians.

6. Why do scholars dispute the integrity of 2 Corinthians and propose it is a composite made up of several different letters?

7. Match each passage from 2 Corinthians with the proper reference:

4.4	We don't proclaim ourselves, you see, but Jesus the Messiah as Lord, and ourselves as your servants because of Jesus.
4.5	What's happening there is that the god of this world has blinded the minds of unbelievers, so that they won't see the light of the gospel of the glory of the Messiah, who is God's image.
5.19–21	Someone I know in the Messiah, fourteen years ago (whether in the body or out of the body I don't know, though God knows), was snatched up to the third heaven. I know that this particular 'Someone' (whether in the body or apart from the body I don't know, God knows) – this person was snatched up to paradise, and heard . . . words you can't pronounce, which humans aren't allowed to repeat.
8.1–2	Let me tell you, my dear family, about the grace which God has given to the Macedonian churches. They have been sorely tested by suffering. But the abundance of grace which was given to them, and the depths of poverty they have endured, have overflowed in a wealth of sincere generosity on their part.
12.2–4	The grace of King Jesus the Lord, the love of God, and the fellowship of the spirit be with you all.
13.13	This is how it came about: God was reconciling the world to himself in the Messiah, not counting their transgressions against them, and entrusting us with the message of reconciliation. So we are ambassadors, speaking on behalf of the Messiah, as though God were making his appeal through us. We implore people on the Messiah's behalf to be reconciled to God. The Messiah did not know sin, but God made him to be sin on our behalf, so that in him we might embody God's faithfulness to the covenant.

8. Read 2 Corinthians 3. What is new in the 'new covenant'?

9. Write an outline of 2 Corinthians.

22

Romans

1. Which of the following do you think best describes Paul's letter to the Romans?

    a. Paul's attempt at systematic theology.

    b. Paul's first pastoral theology.

    c. Paul's missional theology.

    d. Paul's lengthy fundraising letter.

    e. Paul's template for Reformed dogmatics.

    f. Paul's testament in theological form.

Explain your answer.

2. Romans quiz.

    a. Had Paul ever visited Rome before? YES or NO

    b. In what year did Claudius expel some or all the Jews from Rome? _____

    c. How many chapters are there in Romans? _____

    d. In what year did the Jewish Christians return to Rome? _____

    e. From where did Paul write Romans? _____

    f. In what year did Paul approximately write Romans? _____

g. Who did Paul send to deliver the letter to the Roman churches?
_____

h. What was the name of the scribe to whom Paul probably dictated the letter? _____

i. Who does Paul call 'outstanding among the apostles'? J_____ and A_____.

j. Romans 1.5 and 16.26 both mention the o_____ of f_____.

k. Name five women mentioned in the letter.

3. What is Romans about? Fill in the blanks from the list of words below.

Romans gives us a vision of what Paul thought he was trying to achieve by his _____ _____. He was not an itinerant philosopher out to make a quick profit. Nor was he selling a kind of messianic-faith as a '_____' option for gentiles looking for a new religious option. He was certainly not trying to add one more deity to the already overcrowded _____ of Roman gods and goddesses. No, Paul believed that it was his _____, a very Jewish vocation, rooted in Israel's scriptures, to announce that the promises and purposes of Israel's God had been fulfilled, overcoming the dark powers of evil and thus enabling idol-worshipping, sexually immoral, and ritually impure gentiles to come into the transformative '_____ ___ _____'. Thus, by fulfilling Israel's scriptures, the 'gentiles might glorify God for his mercy', while Jews like Paul himself could celebrate the world-changing achievements of Israel's true _____.

pantheon, apostolic labours, obedience of faith, Messiah, vocation, Judaism-lite

4. What are Paul's two favourite Old Testament texts to demonstrate the conformity of his gospel to the pattern of scripture?

Habakkuk _____
Genesis _____

5. What is 'God's righteousness'?

    a. The imputation of the active obedience of Jesus that fulfils a covenant of works that is differentiated from a covenant of grace, which itself is an expression of the binitarian *pactum salutis*, and enabling the elect to be *simul iustus et peccator*.

    b. God's love for the world made known in each and every religion.

    c. God's own in-the-right-ness, his faithfulness to both covenant and creation.

    d. God's work of moral renewal in the hearts of believers, received through the sacraments, and expressed in works of charity.

6. Romans 9–11 is an extended excursus in the letter.

TRUE or FALSE

7. Romans 15.7–13 is the true climax of the letter.

AGREE or DISAGREE

Why?

8. Write an outline of Romans.

23

The Pastoral Epistles

1. What do you think best describes 1–2 Timothy and Titus: pastoral letters or mentoring letters? Explain your answer.

2. What is the significance of the Pauline letter collection ending with these three letters?

3. Pastoral Letters quiz.

    a.   Where was Titus when Paul wrote to him?

    b.   Where was Timothy when Paul wrote to him?

c. Paul wrote all three of these letters from prison in Rome.

    TRUE or FALSE

d. How many chapters are there in 1 Timothy? _____

e. Paul invented the word *heterodidaskaleō*, which means what?

f. About what two individuals did Paul say, 'I have handed over to Satan to be taught not to blaspheme' (1 Tim 1.20 NIV)?

4. Why do some scholars doubt that Paul wrote all of these letters?

5. Match each letter with its proper description:

1 Timothy	Urges Titus to remain in Crete, to continue to instruct the young church, and to assist Zenas and Apollos on their travels. It requests that Titus winter with Paul in Nicopolis.
2 Timothy	An encouragement to Timothy to remain in Ephesus and to establish the orderliness and orthodoxy of the assembly.
Titus	The letter is Paul's 'testament', and asks Timothy to keep the faith, to join him in Rome, and to bring John Mark with him.

6. Write an outline of 1 Timothy, 2 Timothy, and Titus.

VI

THE GOSPELS AND THE STORY OF GOD

The Trinity and the four evangelists from the *Bible historíale* of Charles of France, *c.* AD 1420, held in Paris

24

The Gospel according to Mark

1. The gospel of Mark is essentially a passion story with an extended introduction.

AGREE or DISAGREE

Why?

2. According to tradition, who was Mark?

 a. A Roman equestrian, Marcus Quintus, who came to faith in Christ during Peter's visit to Rome.
 b. A Syrian tax collector named Marcus Cicero Otho who composed the memoirs of the apostle Andrew.
 c. Paul's travelling companion John Mark who wrote the gospel based on Peter's memories.

3. In terms of genre, Mark's gospel most closely resembles which of the following?

    a. An ancient biography.
    b. An ancient tragedy.
    c. An ancient novel.
    d. An ancient comedy.

4. What is the purpose of Mark's gospel?

    a. To explain why nobody thought Jesus was the Messiah until after his resurrection.
    b. To serve as an apology for a crucified Messiah.
    c. To clarify the meaning of the Christ event and discipleship to Jesus in a threatening, confused, and conflicted situation.
    d. To provide a Pauline-friendly version of the Jesus story to counter the Jerusalem church.

5. Where was Mark's gospel written?

    a. Rome
    b. Syria
    c. Decapolis
    d. Ephesus
    e. unsure

6. What is the major turning point in the story of Mark's gospel?

7. *What* does Mark want readers to believe about Jesus, and *how* does he want them to respond to Jesus?

8. Write an outline of Mark's gospel.

25

The Gospel according to Matthew

1. Why do you think the gospel according to Matthew was the most popular book in the first centuries of the church?

2. Where was Matthew likely written?

a. In a Greek-speaking urban centre in Syro-Palestine, among a network of churches that included Jews and gentiles, in proximity to a sizeable Jewish community influenced by pharisaic-rabbinic leaders.

b. In an Aramaic village in the Transjordan long after the Judean revolt against Rome, written to oppose the newly formed Ebionite church and to counter radical Paulinists.

c. In the city of Alexandria as part of a platonic adaptation of the faith that tried to subtly remove or mitigate the influence of Judaism on the early church.

3. Name and describe the five major discourses in Matthew's gospel.

    a. Matthew 5–7:

    b. Matthew 10:

    c. Matthew 13:

    d. Matthew 18:

    e. Matthew 23–25:

4. Matthew wanted the church to hold together both the old and the new.

AGREE or DISAGREE

Why?

5. Read Matthew 10.5–6; 15.24; and 28.19–20. Why did Jesus restrict his ministry to Israel but then tell the apostles to proclaim the gospel to the whole world?

6. Why did Matthew write his gospel? Fill in the blanks from the list of words below.

So why did Matthew write his book? Clearly, to draw out the _____ ways in which the story of Jesus of Nazareth brought the long and _____ story of Israel to its God-ordained goal. This would mean simultaneously offering a manifesto for Jewish believers to retain their _____ to their ancestral scriptures and controlling narrative, and outlining the way in which they should also embrace the new world in which Jesus had been revealed as Israel's Messiah and as the _____, the living embodiment of Israel's God. This would also mean effectively offering an _____, before the watching Jewish world, for following Jesus, presenting this as the fulfilment of Israel's heritage, the true form of _____ to Israel's ancestral calling and hopes.

prophecy-laden, allegiance, manifold, loyalty, Emmanuel, apology

7. Write an outline of the gospel of Matthew.

26

The Gospel according to Luke and Acts of the Apostles

1. Why do you think that Christians with an interest in justice, the Holy Spirit, and preaching all find in Luke-Acts a great resource for their faith?

2. Lucan quiz.

    a.   What percentage of the New Testament does Luke-Acts comprise?

    b.   To whom did Luke write both books?

    c.   What passage is known as the 'Nazareth Manifesto'?

d. Luke is the only evangelist who mentions Martha.

   TRUE or FALSE

e. Luke has two versions of the ascension story.

   TRUE or FALSE

f. What was the name of the slave girl who forgot to open the door to let Peter in?

g. Name the evangelist who had four unmarried daughters who prophesied.

h. Identify one parable unique to Luke's gospel.

i. Name the centurion who was responsible for taking Paul to Rome.

j. When is the first 'we' passage in Acts?

3. How is Luke traditionally identified?

   a. As a gentile, Paul's travelling companion, a doctor.
   b. As a Jerusalem priest who joined the Jerusalem church.
   c. As a second-century gentile Christian from elite circles.
   d. As Lucius of Cyrene, a leader in the church at Antioch.

4. What is the primary theme of Luke-Acts?

    a. Jesus the Messiah and Stephen the martyr.

    b. Why the Lord Jesus didn't return and what the church should do now.

    c. The fulfillment of scripture in the offer of salvation, through Jesus, to the world.

    d. The transition from Jewish sect into early Catholicism.

5. Acts is better read ahead of the New Testament epistles than after the four canonical gospels.

AGREE or DISAGREE

Why?

6. What is the purpose of Luke-Acts? Fill in the blanks from the list of words below.

While Luke-Acts has several utilities, didactic, polemical, and evangelistic, it is principally an _____ work. Luke's gospel _____ and _____ Jesus, while Acts presents Paul as a divinely chosen agent, a faithful herald of Jesus Christ, warmly received by Jewish Christian leaders like _____, slandered and menaced by Jews, and treated _____ by Roman officials. In Luke's narration, the church is radical but harmless, the proper heirs of Judaism's religious _____. Luke engages in a form of ethnic reasoning that legitimates the multi-ethnic churches as God's new covenant people. In the end, Christians retain what pagans _____ about Judaism (antiquity, homogeneity, monotheism, and ethics), while jettisoning what pagans found _____ about Judaism (ethnic-based social separation and strange customs).

extols, apologetic, James, heritage, exonerates, respected, unattractive, unfairly

7. The Acts of the Apostles should be called 'The Acts of the Holy Spirit through the Apostles and Mostly Despite Them'.

AGREE or DISAGREE

Why?

8. Write out an outline of Luke and Acts.

The Gospel according to John

1. Why is John ordinarily called the 'spiritual gospel'? Do you agree or disagree with such a designation? Why?

2. Johannine quiz.

    a.   How many chapters are there in John's gospel? _____

    b.   Name the Judean leader who came to Jesus by night.

    c.   Name seven 'signs' from John's gospel.

d. Name seven 'I am' sayings from John's gospel.

e. Name one story unique to John's gospel.

f. How many exorcisms does Jesus perform in John's gospel? _____

g. In what chapter of John's gospel does Jesus institute the Lord's Supper?
_____

h. How many times does Jesus visit Jerusalem in John's gospel?
_____

3. We could say, thematically speaking, that John was writing a new
g_____, a new e_____, and about p_____.

4. Is the 'beloved disciple' the same person as the apostle John, the brother of James?

YES or NO

5. In what city is John's gospel traditionally thought to have been written?

a. Pisidian Antioch
b. Pergamum
c. Jerusalem
d. Ephesus

6. List the ways that the gospel of John is similar to and different from the synoptic gospels.

Similar	Different

7. According to John 20.31, what is the purpose of John's gospel?

8. Write an outline of John's gospel.

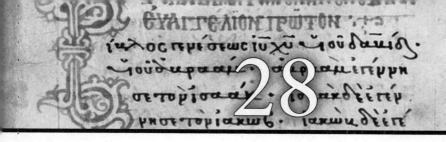

The Making of the Gospels

1. Read Luke 1.1–4. Describe in your own words how Luke gathered the sources to write his gospel.

2. In what way are the gospels similar to Greco-Roman biographies?

3. What best describes John's relationship to the synoptic gospels:

    a. Completely independent of them.

    b. Literary dependence on one or more of them.

    c. Interlocking traditions at an oral stage of the Jesus tradition.

    d. John knows about them, has read at least Mark, follows the same outline and fills in some gaps, but doesn't really use them.

4. Draw a diagram of the Griesbach hypothesis for the synoptic problem.

5. Draw a diagram of the four-source theory for the synoptic problem.

6. Draw a diagram of the Farrer theory for the synoptic problem.

7. What three examples from 1 Corinthians show Paul citing the Jesus tradition to address pastoral and practical problems in the churches in Corinth?

8. Why are the gospels the way that they are? Fill in the blanks from the words provided.

The gospels, then, are not like what we might now have if someone had been able to follow Jesus around Judea and Galilee, filming him with a _____. Rather, the gospels are more like a _____, the recollection and _____ of a significant past, a past only available through the _____ memory of Jesus as it was _____ in the early church. There was undoubtedly some _____ of the Jesus tradition. Jesus' words, and many stories from his public career, were told and retold to _____ and direct the life of the church and to guide it in its _____.

documentary-drama, refraction, undergird, memorization, smartphone, corporate, struggles, transmitted

VII

THE EARLY
CHRISTIANS AND THE
MISSION OF GOD

Icon of the Twelve Apostles
Public Domain

29

Introduction to Early Christian Letters

1. Which is your favourite of the Catholic Letters? Why?

2. In the ancient world, letter writing was largely a substitute for p_____ presence.

3. Match the letters with their types:

Romans	parenetic letter
James; 1 Peter	diaspora letters
Ephesians; 1 John	letter of commendation
Philemon; 3 John	letter of rebuke
2 Peter	protreptic discourse
Galatians	letter of warning
Philippians; 2 John	circular letters
Jude	letters of friendship

4. Why are the Catholic Letters called 'Catholic'?

    a. They were written by the first bishops of the Roman Catholic Church.

    b. They were all written by apostles who led churches.

    c. They exhibit a valuable blend of pastoral assurance and moral exhortation that transcends their original audiences.

    d. They exhibit a distinctive respect for the unity and authority of the one holy catholic and apostolic church.

5. List twelve common themes that characterize the Catholic Letters as a distinct collection:

30

The Letter to the Hebrews

1. 'Jesus is better!' is an adequate summary of Hebrews.

AGREE or DISAGREE

Why?

2. Who wrote Hebrews?

    a. Paul

    b. Luke

    c. Apollos

    d. Priscilla

    e. Only the Lord knows!

3. Should Hebrews be dated before or after the destruction of the Jerusalem temple? Why?

4. What is the purpose of Hebrews?

   a. To persuade gentile believers to add some Jewish practices to their daily routines and religious behaviour.
   b. To persuade Jewish Christians not to go back to the forms of Jewish life that did not acknowledge Jesus as Messiah.
   c. To persuade new believers that unless they try harder to follow Jesus, they could lose their salvation.
   d. To persuade a struggling congregation to persevere in the faith by learning the allegorical significance of the furniture in the temple.

5. The book of Hebrews teaches that it is possible to lose one's salvation.

AGREE or DISAGREE

Why?

6. What does the author of Hebrews consider to be an 'anchor for the soul'?

7. Jesus is better. Match each topic with the correct reference from the book of Hebrews:

sacrifice	4.15
hope	7.19
word	7.22
promise	8.6
high priest	9.23
resurrection	10.34
country	11.16
possession	11.35
covenant	12.24

8. Write an outline of Hebrews.

Letters by Jesus' Brothers: James and Jude

1. Martin Luther called James an 'epistle of straw'. Do you think he was right? Why or why not?

2. Write an outline of James.

3. According to tradition, who was James?

    a. The brother of the Lord.
    b. The Just.
    c. The first bishop of Jerusalem.
    d. A martyr.
    e. All of the above.

4. In what year was James the brother of the Lord martyred, and under what Judean high priest?

5. In what ways does the letter of James reflect Jesus traditions?

6. Identify who wrote these words, James or Paul (all texts NIV):

    a. '[God] chose to give us birth through the word of truth, that we might be a kind of firstfruits of all he created.' _____
    b. 'Faith comes from hearing the message, and the message is heard through the word about Christ.' _____
    c. 'For the entire law is fulfilled in keeping this one command: "Love your neighbor as yourself."' _____
    d. 'If you really keep the royal law found in Scripture, "Love your neighbor as yourself," you are doing right.' _____

7. Why did James write his letter?

8. Why did Jude write his letter?

9. What extra-biblical sources did Jude cite in his letter?

10. Describe the main features of the opponents referred to in Jude.

11. What do the letters of James and Jude have in common? Fill in the gaps from the list of words below.

James and Jude share a common commitment to describe Jesus, their brother, as God's long-awaited _____ _____ _____. Jesus had taught the way of God in _____ and _____, and now exercises _____ over God's gathered people. He will come again to put all things _____.

lordship, wisdom, agent of deliverance, righteousness, right

Petrine Letters:
1 and 2 Peter

1. If you could ask the apostle Peter one question, what would it be?

2. Why do some scholars doubt that Peter wrote 1 Peter? Do you agree or disagree with them? Why?

3. First Peter is addressed to churches in the regions of P_____, G_____, C_____, A_____, and B_____.

4. Explain the reasons 1 Peter might have been written to either a Jewish or a gentile audience:

Jewish audience	gentile audience

5. In terms of genre, 1 Peter is a d_____ letter.

6. What is the purpose of 1 Peter?

    a. To warn Christians in Asia Minor about the apostle Paul and his antinomian gospel.

    b. To exhort Christians in Asia Minor to maintain their faith amid social scorn, shaming, slander, and stigma.

    c. To urge Christians to pray for Peter as he approaches his forthcoming martyrdom in Rome.

    d. To exhort Christians in Asia Minor to defend the faith against apostates and heretics who distort the faith as a licence for sin.

7. Write an outline of 1 Peter.

8. Why do some scholars doubt that Peter wrote 2 Peter? Do you agree or disagree with them? Why?

9. Describe the five features which characterize the false teachers spoken about in the letter.

10. What is the purpose of 2 Peter?

    a. To oppose a general tide of philosophies and heresies that has either infiltrated the church or might draw people away from the church.

    b. To explain why the return of the Lord will be very soon and will lead to the renovation of the created order.

    c. To reinforce the authority and legacy of Peter as true custodian of apostolic tradition over and against the apostolates of Paul, James, and John.

    d. To urge the churches to accept the letters of Jude and Paul as authentic and authoritative.

11. Write an outline of 2 Peter.

Johannine Letters:
1, 2, and 3 John

1. What do you think is the dominating theme across the Johannine letters?

    a. love

    b. atonement

    c. testimony

    d. truth

    e. all of the above

2. Who is John the elder?

    a. The same person as John the apostle.

    b. A different John, the one to whom Papias referred.

    c. The same person as John the evangelist who wrote the gospel, but not John the apostle.

    d. I am not sure.

3. In what ways are the Johannine letters similar to the gospel of John?

4. Match each Johannine letter with its proper description:

1 John — A covering letter to a specific but unknown church, in which the elder writes on behalf of the 'children of your elect sister' to the 'elect lady' (likely metaphors for two sister churches), urging them to watch out for, and to refuse hospitality to, certain deceivers and anti-Christs who were teaching docetism.

2 John — A circular pastoral letter to churches in Asia Minor, rooted in the elder's preaching, reinforcing christological boundaries against the teaching of the secessionists.

3 John — A personal letter from the elder to Gaius, probably a leader and ally in the church that received the other two letters. The writer is warning Gaius about Diotrephes and the threat he poses.

5. John the elder was fighting on two fronts. First, against those who denied that Jesus was the M_____. Second, against those who denied that Jesus came in the f_____.

6. What does the heresy of docetism deny?

    a. That Jesus had a human soul.
    b. That Jesus was the Messiah.
    c. That Jesus was God's Son.
    d. That Jesus had a human body.

7. What passage or verse best sums up the Johannine letters?

    a. 'That which was from the beginning, which we have heard, which we have seen with our eyes, which we have gazed at, and our hands have handled – concerning the Word of Life! That life was displayed, and we have seen it, and bear witness, and we announce to you the life of God's coming age, which was with the father and was displayed to us.

That which we have seen and heard, we announce to you too, so that you also may have fellowship with us. And our fellowship is with the father, and with his son Jesus the Messiah. We are writing these things so that our joy may be complete' (1 John 1.1–4).

b. 'Children, it is the last hour. You have heard that "Antimessiah" is coming – and now many Antimessiahs have appeared! That's how we know that it is the last hour. They went out from among us, but they were not really of our number. If they had been of our number, you see, they would have remained with us. This happened so that it would be made crystal clear that none of them belonged to us' (1 John 2.18–19).

c. 'This is what makes love complete for us, so that we may have boldness and confidence on the day of judgment, because just as he is, so are we within this world' (1 John 4.17).

d. 'I am writing these things to you so that you may know that you, who believe in the name of the son of God, do indeed have the life of the age to come' (1 John 5.13).

e. I think they all are good!

8. Write an outline of 1 John.

34

Revelation

1. 'Revelation is not about timetables, it's about testimony; the focus is not on an eschatological forecast of the future, but faithfulness in the shadow of empire.'

AGREE or DISAGREE

Why?

2. Why do some scholars suspect that John of Patmos is not the same person as John the apostle?

3. Revelation is often dated to the reign of the Roman emperor D_____.

4. In terms of genre, the book of Revelation combines features of a l_____, a p_____, and an a_____.

5. What is an apocalypse? Fill in the blanks with the words provided below.

An apocalypse, according to one definition, 'is a genre of _____ literature with a narrative framework, in which a revelation is mediated by an _____ being to a human recipient, disclosing a _____ reality which is both temporal, insofar as it envisages eschatological salvation, and _____, insofar as it involves another supernatural world . . . intended to _____ present, earthly circumstances in light of the supernatural world of the future, and to influence both the understanding and the behaviour of the audience by means of _____ _____.'

revelatory, transcendent, interpret, spatial, otherworldly, divine authority

6. The seven churches in Revelation are: E_____, S_____, P_____, T_____, S_____, P_____, and L_____.

7. Match the designation with the description of the four major interpretive approaches to Revelation:

preterist

Regards Revelation as a multi-layered symbolic portrayal of the conflict taking place between the kingdom of God and the kingdoms of this world in the time between the victory of Jesus on the cross and his final return.

historicist

Looks for a specific fulfilment of the prophecies of the book in actual events that have now already happened, with some fixing on the events leading up to the fall of Jerusalem in AD 70 and others supposing that fulfilment came in the fourth-century collapse of the pagan Roman Empire and its Christianisation under Constantine.

futurist

Regards Revelation as predicting long-range future events, except that the 'history' in question begins in what, for us, is the 'modern' period.

idealist

Supposes that the author was predicting the entire course of subsequent world history, including things like the rise of the Goths, the Arabs, the Mongols, the medieval papacy, Napoleon, Hitler, and the Soviet Union.

8. Read this statement:

John's pastoral purpose is as much to exhort his hearers to endurance as to assure them of God's ultimate victory over their adversaries. He therefore provides a God's-eye view of the plight of the Asian churches and explains how Jesus' people are destined to reign with him in the new creation. Along the way there are exhortations and prophecies, warnings and judgments, triumphs mixed with tears, old adversaries and a new world. For all the (to us) vagueness of John's vision, and the vagaries of his language, the book of Revelation gives its audience the confidence and hope that the Lamb has triumphed, and will yet triumph, over the evils of the world.

AGREE or DISAGREE

Why?

9. To what extent does understanding Revelation require a solid grasp of the Old Testament? Give a concrete example from the book.

10. Write an outline of Revelation.

VIII

THE MAKING
OF THE
NEW TESTAMENT

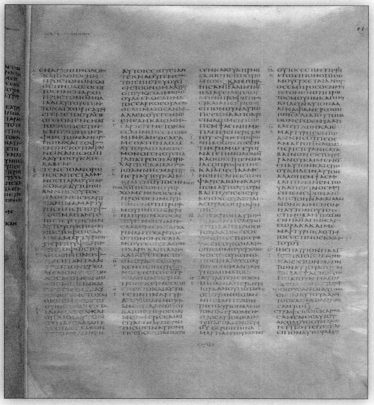

John 1.1–18, Codex Sinaiticus

Introduction to Textual Criticism of the New Testament

1. If someone asked you, 'Where did the Bible come from?' what would you say?

2. Create a flow chart showing the relationship between the entities below to create an English Bible.

English Bible, first copyists, medieval manuscripts, ancient manuscripts, critical editions of Greek and Hebrew Bibles, biblical author, collections of manuscripts, translator(s) of Greek New Testament and Hebrew Old Testament.

3. What is the goal of textual criticism?

    a. To identify the first canonical edition of the New Testament made in the mid to late second century.

    b. To unpack the living process of textual transmission, the historical and theological forces that shaped textual transmission, and the impact that textual variations had on the theology of the churches.

    c. To identify, as far as possible, the initial text, which itself stands in some relationship to an original autograph.

4. Match each material used in textual criticism with its description:

papyri	The different languages into which the New Testament was translated. This includes Latin, Syriac, Coptic, Armenian, Georgian, Ethiopic, Arabic, Slavonic, Gothic, and more.
majuscules	Papyrus sheets, either scrolls or small codices.
minuscules	Script which employs capital letters with no spaces between words.
versions	Scripture which employs lower-case letters with spaces between words.
patristic quotations	Church writings that contain a sequence of yearly readings for use in the liturgy.
lectionaries	Citations of the New Testament from the church fathers.

5. Match the evidence used to evaluate the textual variants with the proper descriptions:

External Evidence		Internal Evidence	
Date of witnesses	A reading is preferred if it has coherence with textual witnesses whose ancestor was the initial text; whereas a reading has poor 'coherence' if it is found only among texts that are distantly related to an initial text.	The more difficult reading is to be preferred.	A reading is preferred if it was potentially embarrassing to the theological proclivities of some copyists.
Geographical distribution of witnesses	Appeals to geographically diversified sources.	The shorter reading is to be preferred.	A reading is preferred if it coheres with the style and vocabulary of an author and the literary context of a passage, and if it does not look like harmonizations or improvements.
Genealogical coherence	Preference is generally given to earlier witnesses, usually the papyri, though often the major majuscules.	Contextual considerations	Shorter readings are preferred because a scribe was more likely to expand a text than reduce it.
		Explanatory power	A reading is preferred if it explains and accounts for not only the passage in question but also the other variants.

6. What are the *ECM*, NA (28), UBS (5), *SBLGNT*, and *THGNT* all types of?

    a. Discount codes for Christian dating websites.

    b. Names of ancient manuscripts.

    c. Abbreviations for English Bible translations.

    d. Abbreviations for critical editions of the Greek New Testament.

The Canonization
of the New Testament

1. The Bible was created and canonized by:

    a. A secret society called the Illuminati who concocted the whole thing and sent copies to every monastery in medieval Europe in the sixth century.

    b. St. Pelagius the Pugnacious after chairing the council of Serdica in the fifth century.

    c. The Roman emperor Constantine with a group of bishops in the fourth century.

    d. A gradual process of discussion and debate that climaxed in the fourth century.

2. By AD 200 which books were unanimously considered part of the church's sacred texts, faith, and worship?

3. Which books were 'disputed' when it came to inclusion in the canon?

4. What other Christian writings were popular and were considered for canonization?

5. Match each criterion with its description:

apostolicity

Texts were accepted if they comported with the apostolic proclamation which crystallized into the rule of faith.

orthodoxy

Writings close to the time of Jesus and the apostles, even if not strictly by apostles themselves, were still candidates for acceptance.

antiquity

Writings were accepted if they were recognized by a wide geographical distribution of churches.

catholicity

A text was more likely to be accepted if it was attributed to an apostle or to one of the apostle's associates, and if it actually looked like an apostolic document as opposed to a forgery.

IX

LIVING THE STORY OF THE NEW TESTAMENT

Fresco of banquet scene, Catacombe dei Santi Marcellino e Pietro, Rome, Italy, dated fourth century

De Agostini Picture Library / Bridgeman Images

37

Bringing It All Together

1. What is the purpose of studying the New Testament?

    a. To make sure we know how to vote the right way.

    b. To help us obey all of the commands God imposes on us.

    c. To enable us to live out the story of Jesus and the early church in our dramatic performance in our own time and place.

    d. To maintain a proper distinction between law and gospel.

2. Learning about the New Testament helps us answer several basic questions that make up a world view, including:

    a. W_____ are we?

    b. W_____ are we?

    c. W_____ is wrong?

    d. H_____ is this to be put right?

    e. W_____ time is it?

3. Consider this statement:

The New Testament thus provides the basis for a theology and a world view in which we can explain and enact, under the guidance of the Spirit, several things universal to human experience: justice, spirituality, relationships, beauty, freedom, truth, and power.

AGREE or DISAGREE

Why?

4. What is the mission of the church?

In what sense is it holistic?

How does it depend on unity and holiness?

5. Describe in what sense Christian life is a pilgrimage.

6. What verse of scripture do you think best sums up Christian hope?

7. After reading *The New Testament in Its World* and utilizing the workbook, describe the following:

The biggest 'aha' moment you had.

Your biggest disagreement with the book.

The strangest thing you read in the book.

The funniest thing you read in the book.

The wisest thing you read in the book.